P9-DUT-904

# CHIMPANZEE

SAMANTHA BELL

Published in the United States of America by Cherry Lake Publishing
Ann Arbor, Michigan
www.cherrylakepublishing.com

Content Adviser: John Mitani, Primate Behavioral Ecologist, University of Michigan and Ngogo Chimpanzee Project
Reading Adviser: Marla Conn, ReadAbility, Inc.

Photo Credits: ©Patrick Rolands/Shutterstock Images, cover, 1, 11; ©Stephen Meese/Shutterstock Images, 5; ©UNEP-WCMC and IUCN (International Union for Conservation of Nature) 2008, 6; ©Sergey Uryadnikov/Shutterstock Images, 7, 13, 25, 27; ©Alan Jeffery/Shutterstock Images, 8; ©Dorling Kindersley/Thinkstock, 12; ©Aaron Amat/ Shutterstock Images, 15; ©Sam DCruz/Shutterstock Images, 17; ©Vincentstthomas/Dreamstime.com, 19; ©LMPphoto/Shutterstock Images, 21; ©Anup Shah/Thinkstock, 23; ©Robin Nieuwenkamp/Shutterstock Images, 29

Library of Congress Cataloging-in-Publication Data

Bell, Samantha, author.
Chimpanzee / by Samantha Bell
    pages cm. — (Exploring our rainforests)
  Summary: "Introduces facts about chimpanzees, including physical features, habitat, life cycle, food, and threats to these rainforest creatures. Photos, captions, and keywords supplement the narrative of this informational text." — Provided by publisher.
  Audience: Ages 8-12.
  Audience: Grades 4 to 6.
  ISBN 978-1-63188-974-5 (hardcover) — ISBN 978-1-63362-013-1 (pbk.) — ISBN 978-1-63362-052-0 (pdf) — ISBN 978-1-63362-091-9 (ebook) 1. Chimpanzees—Juvenile literature. I. Title.

QL737.P94B45 2014
599.885—dc23                                    2014020995

Cherry Lake Publishing would like to acknowledge the work of
The Partnership for 21st Century Skills. Please visit www.p21.org
for more information.

Printed in the United States of America
Corporate Graphics

## ABOUT THE AUTHOR

Samantha Bell lives in South Carolina with her husband, four children, and lots of animals. She has written and/or illustrated more than 20 books for children. She loves being outdoors and learning about all the amazing wonders of nature.

# TABLE OF CONTENTS

# CHAPTER 1

# WHAT GREAT APES!

Quickly the chimpanzees move from tree to tree. Just ahead is a tree filled with figs, the small, sweet fruit that chimps eat. After filling up, the chimps walk across branches through the rainforest, finally reaching their nests high in the trees for a nap.

In the wild, chimpanzees live in **communities** and use natural objects as tools. Once in a while, they will stand upright and walk on two legs. In **captivity**, chimps learn to use sign language and star in movies. They are smart and curious, but also strong and aggressive. Like gorillas and orangutans, chimps are great apes.

Chimpanzees are divided into two species, the chimpanzee and the bonobo. Chimpanzees are divided into four subspecies. Each subspecies lives in a different region of Africa. Bonobos live near the Congo River in central Africa.

*Chimpanzees sometimes walk on two legs, and sometimes on all fours.*

# RANGE MAP

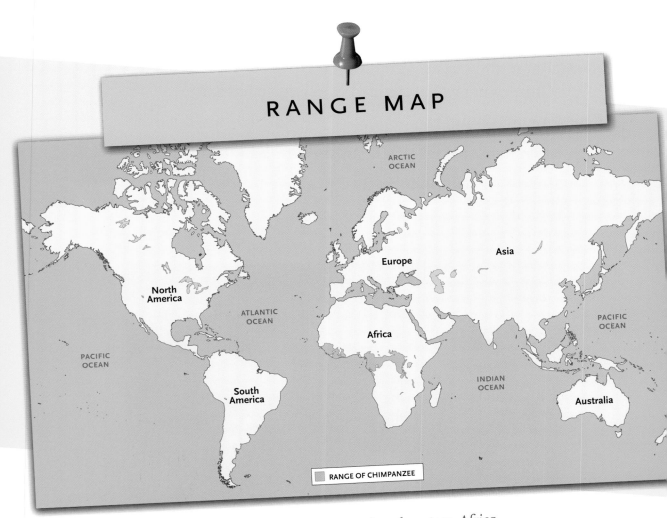

ARCTIC OCEAN

Europe

Asia

North America

ATLANTIC OCEAN

PACIFIC OCEAN

PACIFIC OCEAN

Africa

South America

INDIAN OCEAN

Australia

RANGE OF CHIMPANZEE

*Chimpanzees live in central and western Africa.*

[ 21ST CENTURY SKILLS LIBRARY ]

Many chimpanzees live in the tropical rainforests. As the forests are being cut down, however, some chimpanzees have had to adapt to other habitats. Today they can be found in mountain forests, bamboo forests, swamp forests, and even open **savannas**. Most depend on the trees for places to eat and sleep.

*These bonobos live near a swamp.*

*Chimpanzees groom their friends and relatives.*

Chimpanzees, or chimps, are social animals. They live in communities with 20 to 200 other chimps. Each community has a **home range**, and the chimps move about the range in small groups. Males will spend their whole lives in the same community where they were born. They have a social **hierarchy**, which means that some males have a higher rank than others. The males are also **dominant** over all the females in the group. To show their dominance, male chimps will slap the ground, stomp their feet, or throw rocks. Many females don't stay in the same community. When they are about 11 years old, they will leave their home range to join another group.

One way the chimps in the community build relationships is by **grooming**. The chimps spend time each day removing dirt and ticks, very small insects, from each other's hair. As they groom, they make a variety of sounds such as lip-smacking and tooth-clacking.

## THINK ABOUT IT

CHIMPS GROOM EACH OTHER TO BUILD RELATIONSHIPS IN THEIR COMMUNITY. WHAT ARE SOME WAYS PEOPLE BUILD RELATIONSHIPS WITH FAMILY MEMBERS? WITH FRIENDS?

# CHAPTER 2

# WALKING THE WALK

Full-grown chimps stand about 4 feet (1.2 meters) tall, about the same height as a 6-year-old boy. In the wild, chimps weigh from 70 to 130 pounds (31.8 to 59 kilograms), and they can grow even larger in captivity. An adult chimp has five or six times the strength of a human being!

Chimpanzees are covered with black or dark brown hair. The palms of their hands and soles of their feet don't have any hair. Chimps don't have hair on their faces or ears, either.

Like people, chimps can walk upright on two legs. They usually move around on all fours, however. Instead of walking on the palms of their hands, they curl their fingers in and "walk" on their knuckles. A chimpanzee's arms are longer than its legs, so when it knuckle-walks, its head and front end are higher than its back end.

*Because they're so strong, chimpanzees are able to climb trees easily.*

# BODY DIAGRAM

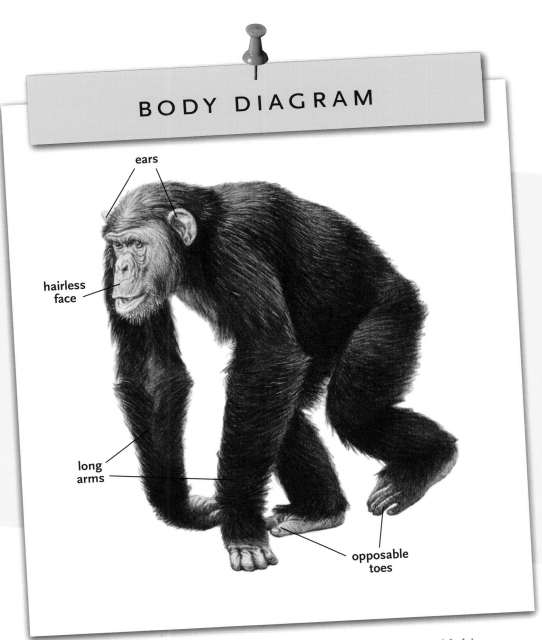

ears

hairless
face

long
arms

opposable
toes

*Chimpanzees have opposable thumbs and toes to help them hold things.*

*Bonobos' arms are perfect for life in the trees.*

Chimps also use their arms to swing through the trees. They have long hands and fingers with short thumbs. This lets them use their hands like hooks when moving from branch to branch. Their thumbs are **opposable**, allowing them to grasp and pick up objects. Chimps also have opposable toes. Their big toes work like thumbs, helping them hold onto branches and climb trees quickly.

Chimps communicate with one another a lot like humans do. They hug, kiss, hold hands, pat one another on the back, and even tickle one another. An angry chimp may stand upright and wave its arms. A chimp that is upset or begging for something will pout. If the chimp is afraid, it will often smile, showing its teeth. This "grin of fear" is a lot like a human's nervous smile when a situation is awkward or uncomfortable.

Chimpanzees communicate with sounds, too. They make more than 30 different sounds to tell other chimps how they feel. Happy and excited chimps laugh, pant, or smack their lips. Chimpanzees that are upset may cry or whimper. Each chimp also makes a panting-hooting sound that is all his or her own. Each chimp can be recognized by this sound. Even if it comes from across the forest, the other chimps know who is making this call.

*Chimpanzees show their sharp teeth when upset.*

## LOOK AGAIN

### LOOK CLOSELY AT THIS PHOTOGRAPH OF A CHIMP COMMUNICATING. HOW WOULD YOU DESCRIBE THIS CHIMP'S MOOD?

— CHAPTER 3 —

# CHIMPS AS CHEFS

Chimpanzees spend most of their time moving from one food source to another. As **omnivores**, they enjoy lots of variety in their diets. While in the trees, chimps eat fruits, seeds, nuts, bark, buds, blossoms, and leaves. They also eat insects and eggs, as well as other mammals. Because they eat so many different foods, chimps are able to live in different types of habitats.

When a chimp finds food, it will call the others to let them know the location. Females eat more insects, while male chimpanzees tend to eat more meat. A favorite

*Fruit is a big part of chimpanzees' diet.*

meal could include small monkeys and antelopes. The largest animals that chimps hunt are colobus monkeys, baboons, and bush pigs. Sometimes chimps will capture adult animals, though they usually try to take younger ones. To catch them, the chimps will form a small group that hunts together. They spread out along the ground and in the trees to corner their prey. Then if the prey is caught, the chimps make intense, excited sounds to tell the others.

Not many animals use tools, but chimps do. They use them to collect some of their food. Instead of nets or fishing poles, they use objects like twigs, stems, and grass. Sometimes chimps will shape a stick and use it to dig grubs, or insect larvae, from a log. Other times they will poke a blade of grass into a termite mound. The termites bite the grass, and the chimp pulls them up and eats them. Chimpanzees also use leaves as sponges to soak up water to drink. They smash tasty nuts with rocks or stones.

*This chimpanzee in a zoo is using a stick as a tool to get fruit out of a box.*

Chimpanzees are unusual animals in another way, too. They use special plants as medicines. Usually when chimps eat leaves, they pull them off the branches and chew them up as fast as they can. But with certain plants, chimps will remove the leaves one at a time, roll them around in their mouths, then swallow them whole. The leaves help chimps get rid of **parasites**. Scientists believe some chimps eat dirt for the same reason.

GO DEEPER

SCIENTISTS STUDY THE TYPES OF PLANTS CHIMPANZEES EAT. IN WHAT WAYS CAN THIS HELP PEOPLE WHO ARE SICK?

Chimpanzees are smart enough to know which plants will keep them healthy.

# CHAPTER 4

# CHIMPS IN CHILDHOOD

Eight to 9 months after mating, a female chimp will give birth to just one baby (usually). Newborn chimps are constantly with their mothers. Because the babies are not strong enough to support themselves, the mother must hold them close at all times. Like other mammals, the mother chimp feeds her baby milk. It depends on her for food, warmth, and protection.

As an infant, the chimp rides on its mother's back. By the time the chimp is a year old, it will begin to sit a few yards away from her. It also starts eating by itself and

*Baby chimpanzees depends on their mothers to travel around.*

playing with other chimps. At 2, it begins to wander a little further.

A chimp will usually stop nursing and riding on its mother by age 5. It interacts with members of the community, but still stays close to its mother.

**Adolescent** chimps become more independent. Some females begin moving between groups. Males join others in hunting. They may also keep watch around the borders of the community. Yet even after they are grown, many males still turn to their mothers for comfort and support.

A female can give birth every 3 to 6 years, so she can have young of different ages with her at any time. The bonds between these brothers and sisters are strong. Older siblings sometimes carry and play with infants. If the mother chimp dies, often the older ones will take care of the younger ones. Although males don't help raise the young, they will sometimes play with them.

In the wild, chimpanzees can live up to 60 years. In captivity, they live even longer.

*The baby chimp stays close to its mother at mealtime.*

## LOOK AGAIN

LOOK CLOSELY AT THIS PHOTOGRAPH OF A MOTHER AND HER YOUNG CHIMP. IN WHAT WAYS IS A CHIMPANZEE MOTHER SIMILAR TO A HUMAN MOTHER? IN WHAT WAYS ARE THEY DIFFERENT?

# RAINFOREST DANGER

Chimpanzees don't have many natural enemies. A leopard or lion may eat a chimp, especially a young one. But chimps can be dangerous to one another.

Within a community, males show their power in displays meant to frighten other males. Their hair stands on end so they look bigger. They stamp their feet or scream. They may drag branches and throw rocks. Males try to scare other chimps so they will refuse to fight. If fighting does take place, it can be vicious. A chimp may be seriously hurt or even be killed.

*Bonobos can be fierce during a conflict.*

Sometimes a community of chimpanzees will move in and attack another community. The males purposely try to injure or kill the other chimps. Often the group with the most chimps wins.

Chimpanzees are aware of the danger around them. Groups of males will patrol the edges of the home range to protect it. Chimps also warn one another if they see danger. They will sound an alarm until the other chimps hear the warning and escape to safety.

The biggest threat to chimps' survival, however, comes from humans. People cut down the forests to make room for houses, mines, and farms. They chop down trees to use or sell, and chimps' habitats are destroyed. Chimps are also in danger of catching human diseases. Some chimps are caught and sold illegally as **bushmeat**.

The International Union for the Conservation of Nature (IUCN) lists chimpanzees as **endangered**. They are protected by law throughout their range, but the laws are poorly enforced. There are groups, however, that recognize the need and want to help. Environmental organizations are working on conserving chimps' habitats. Other organizations are getting local residents involved in creating **sanctuaries** and starting educational programs. As more people learn about chimpanzees, these wonderful animals will have a better chance of survival.

*Chimpanzees depend on trees for food and shelter.*

## LOOK AGAIN

Look closely at this photograph of a chimpanzee living in its natural habitat. Do you see natural resources that should be protected from humans?

# THINK ABOUT IT

- Some people keep chimpanzees as pets. If you had the opportunity, would you keep a chimpanzee as a pet? Why or why not?

- Search the Internet with an adult for a video of chimpanzee mothers and infants. Compare the information in this book to information in the video. Does the video include facts that are the same? Are there facts that are different?

- What was the most surprising fact you learned by reading this book? Write down three questions you still have about chimpanzees. Discuss them with a partner or a small group.

# LEARN MORE

## FURTHER READING

Goodall, Jane, and Michael Neugebauer. *The Chimpanzee Family Book*. New York: North-South Books, 1997.

Marsico, Katie. *Chimpanzees*. New York: Scholastic, 2012.

Shaffer, Jody Jensen. *Chimpanzees*. Edina, MN: ABDO, 2014.

## WEB SITES

**The Jane Goodall Institute—Chimpanzees: Communication**
http://www.janegoodall.org/chimpanzees/communication
Watch a video as male chimps display a form of communication showing dominance.

**Lincoln Park Zoo—Chimpanzee**
http://www.lpzoo.org/animals/factsheet/chimpanzee
Watch the fun chimpanzees have as they play in the snow at the Lincoln Park Zoo in Chicago, Illinois.

**National Geographic Kids—Chimpanzee**
http://kids.nationalgeographic.com/kids/animals/creaturefeature/chimpanzee
Enjoy photos of chimpanzees, see a map of where they live, and read more interesting facts.

# GLOSSARY

**adolescent (ad-uh-LES-uhnt)** a teenager; someone in the period of life before adulthood

**bushmeat (BUSH-meet)** the meat of wild animals killed and eaten by native people

**captivity (kap-TIV-i-tee)** the condition of being held or trapped by people

**communities (kuh-MYOO-ni-teez)** groups of living creatures in different areas that interact with one another

**dominant (DAH-muh-nuhnt)** most influential or powerful

**endangered (en-DAYN-jerd)** at risk of dying out

**grooming (GROOM-eng)** making neat, attractive, and acceptable

**hierarchy (HYE-ur-ahr-kee)** an arrangement of people or things in ranks or levels of importance

**home range (HOHM RAYNG)** the area in which an animal normally lives

**omnivores (OM-nuh-vohrz)** animals that eat both plants and other animals

**opposable (uh-POH-zuh-buhl)** capable of being placed against another digit on a hand or foot

**parasites (PAR-uh-sites)** animals or plants that live on or inside of another animal or plant, often causing harm

**sanctuaries (SANGK-choo-er-eez)** natural areas where animals are protected from hunters

**savannas (suh-VAN-uhz)** grasslands with scattered trees

# INDEX